The editors would like to thank
TINA DOLEY CARLSON,
UCLA Certified Mindfulness Facilitator, Semel Institute,
Mindful Awareness Research Center,
for her assistance in the preparation of this book.

Visit us on the Web!
Seussville.com
rhcbooks.com

Educators and librarians, for a variety of teaching tools, visit us at RHTeachersLibrarians.com

Library of Congress Cataloging-in-Publication Data is available upon request.
ISBN 978-0-593-37935-6 (trade) — ISBN 978-0-593-37936-3 (lib. bdg.)

MANUFACTURED IN CHINA

10 9 8 7 6 5 4 3 2 1

First Edition

THE CAT ON THE MAT

by Bonnie Worth

illustrated by Aristides Ruiz and Joe Mathieu

The Cat in the Hat's Learning Library®

Random House 🏠 New York

I'm the Cat on the mat,
and what I plan to do
is talk about mindfulness
meditation with you.

Mindfulness meditation
will help you to see
thoughts, feelings, and senses
and just let them be.

Life's a juggling act
that can make us feel dizzy.
Keeping balls in the air
all the time—busy, busy!

With mindfulness, we learn
to let those balls go—
let them be, just for now
and take time to go slow.

You can sit in a chair
or crisscross on a mat,
back straight, hands still,
and relax, just like that.

We often think of
what's past or ahead.
With mindfulness, we notice
what's NOW instead.

Like boats have their anchors
to keep them from drifting,
we focus on something
so our minds don't keep shifting.

A good way to start—
or so I have found—
is to open your ears
to the wide world of sound!

Whatever you hear,
just let it be there—
whether loud noise or soft. . . .

wwhhhiiirrrrrrrr

chirp
chirp

purrr purrrrr purrrrrrrr

ZZZRRRMMMM

Can you listen to air?

Feel your breath moving
as air comes and goes.
Feel it move in your chest,
belly, throat, mouth, or nose.

Breathe in like a wave that
pulls back from the land.
Breathe out like a wave
as it breaks on the sand.

Ahhhhhh!

Whooosh!

You'll find that your mind
likes to take off and run.
Oh, yes, it is frisky!
It wants to have fun!

Zriiirip!!!

Whenever you notice
your mind's gone astray,
good for you that you noticed.
Yay for you! Hip-hooray!

MIND

Bring the frisky one back,
oh so gently—that's how
your mind learns to stay
in the here and now.

Take time to calm down
and stop wiggling about.
Get still. Feel your body
from INSIDE, not out.

Feel your cheeks. Feel your eyes.
Feel your nose breathing air,
lips and jaws hanging loose.
Feel your skull. Feel your hair!

Feel your shoulders,
your arms, your forearms, and then . . .
feel your hands and your fingers.
Feel each one, all ten!

Feel the length of your thighs
as they end at your knees.
Feel your shins and your feet
and all ten piggies, please.

Sense the spaces within.
You may sense them all day
as you finish this practice
and go on your way.

Dealing with thoughts?

It is no easy task.

What makes it so hard?

It's your mind, since you ask.

Your mind is a chatterbox.

Nonstop, it just chatters.

Saying all sorts of things

(not much of which matters).

So prepare to be mindful,
like you've learned to do.
Watch your thoughts floating past
in the stream next to you.

Label them as they come—
hope, wish, or daydream.
That's all that they are—
just words in a stream.

tomorrow
family
hope
loss
school
now

31

The mindful person,
I do need to mention,
listens and pays
closer attention.

Listens to friends
with an open heart and mind.
It's the kindest of acts.
It is kinder than kind!

Be kind to them all—
whether family or friend.
But be kindest of all
to yourself in the end.

Make friends with yourself—
be the bestest of best!
And your body and mind
will both get a good rest.

In this last meditation
you will be sending out
kindness and love.
That's what it's about!

Imagine someone,
close to you or apart,
and think of their goodness,
down deep in your heart.

Send that someone wishes
and say them like so:
"May you know joy.
May all sadness go."

"May you live life with ease.
May you be free from woe.
May you be strong and wise
wherever you go."

Then turn it around
and send wishes out to
a wonderful someone.
That someone is YOU!

If you say it enough,
I think you'll find that
you'll live a good life . . .

health
wisdom
patience
love

. . . like the Cat on the Mat!

Dear Parents and Caregivers,

Mindfulness is a practice that teaches children to know and be open to what is happening in the present moment. Cultivating the capacity to pay attention and getting to know one's body, heart, and mind are also excellent ways to get in touch with the simple joy of being.

Studies have found that mindfulness benefits include:

- improved attention and focus

- better emotion regulation

- greater empathy

- increased impulse control

- stronger resilience

- more compassion for self and others

- greater sense of well-being

- reduced anxiety, stress, and depression

Some helpful websites for mindfulness are:

The Mindful Awareness Research Center (MARC) at UCLA offers online classes and workshops to the general public, as well as free guided meditations. Aimed at adults, this is a great place to start learning about mindfulness. Visit uclahealth.org/marc/

Mindful Schools specializes in bringing mindfulness to educators and into classrooms, and has wonderful resources explaining mindfulness and citing some of the research supporting its many benefits. Visit mindfulschools.org

FOR FURTHER READING

For children

Breathing Makes It Better: A Book for Sad Days, Mad Days, Glad Days, and All the Feelings In-Between by Christopher Willard and Wendy O'Leary (Bala Kids). This award-winning, interactive picture book shows children how to breathe through their feelings and find calm. For ages 3 and up.

A Handful of Quiet: Happiness in Four Pebbles by Thich Nhat Hanh (Plum Blossom). The author uses four stones to teach the principle of meditation. For ages 5 and up.

For parents and caregivers

Mindful Games: Sharing Mindfulness and Meditation with Children, Teens, and Families by Susan Kaiser Greenland (Shambhala). Includes fifty simple games for parents, caregivers, and teachers to play with children (or adults) to improve focus and mindfulness.

Sitting Still Like a Frog: Mindfulness Exercises for Kids (and Their Parents) by Eline Snel, foreword by Jon Kabat-Zinn (Shambhala). Written by a noted expert, this book of simple mindfulness practices is for parents to use with children ages 5 to 12. It comes with a sixty-minute audio CD of guided exercises.